Jc
Travelbooks for Kids™

Mackinaw

Holland ☆

Frankenmuth

*With special thanks to
the Michigan Chambers of Commerce.*

Cover Picture: Windmill Island, Holland, Michigan.

Jody's Travelbooks for Kids™

Summary: Real-life travel activities for kids,
framed by a story about an adventurous little girl and her big
brother, who wants to grow up to be an historian. The series
is named after Jody the Dutch mouse, who acts as tour guide.

Vol. II, Holland, Michigan, is available from
Paint Creek Press, Ltd.
P.O. Box 80547, Rochester, MI 48308-0001

Printed and bound in the United States of America
by Paint Creek Press, Ltd.

ISBN 0-9648564-8-4

This Whole Thing Started When . . .

my little sister, Katie Murphy, was almost five. Our family went to Holland, Michigan for the Tulip Festival that year. It was really fun until my sister turned it into a disaster.

Katie didn't know about travel diaries then. Two years later, her second-grade teacher told her class about the Italian explorer, Marco Polo. Marco became famous by writing about his trips to China. This inspired Katie to become a "famous tourist."

My name is Kevin, by the way. I love history. I know how to write, plus I'm old enough to use our father, Michael Murphy's laptop computer. Katie figured this would make me the perfect person to be her secretary.

I found out she was planning to give all the credit for our stories to a stupid stuffed mouse named Jody. That's when I told her she had to pay me. I don't work for nothing.

The Frankenmuth trip was the first one I keyboarded. Katie was seven. She liked the story, but not what I said about her. Oh well. After Frankenmuth, I wrote about Holland. That's where Jody the mouse joined our family.

After my sister Katie and I got back from Frankenmuth, Katie introduced Gund the German raccoon to Jody the Dutch mouse. Jody told Gund about the beautiful bright tulips in the land he came from. This reminded Katie of the good times we had when we went to Holland two years ago.

My name is Kevin. My sister calls me "Kevie" when she wants something.

"Kevie," she said in her most sugary voice. "I'm glad we typed the story of our Frankenmuth trip into daddy's laptop computer. Aren't you? Let's write about the tulip festival next. Want to?"

Not. I thought. But, I did like the idea of making money off my sister.

"That's cool." I said out loud. "Just don't forget you promised to hand over your allowance as payment for my services."

Katie gave me a dirty look. Then she sighed. "Okay. If a person wants to do something worthwhile in life, I guess she just has to suffer."

"You have to pay me, Katie, " I warned. "Dad said you have to. A deal's a deal."

"I said okay!"

My mom loves spring. The year Katie turned five, my mom decided we should all go to the tulip festival in Holland, Michigan. Katie was thrilled about the idea. She looked on it as a pre-birthday celebration.

Me, I'm not real big on tulips, but when I looked at the map, I saw that Holland is on the west coast of Michigan. I love the Great Lakes. I was eager to see the sand dunes, the lighthouse, and the really cool boats they have there. My dad had heard there were bike trails all around the place. We took our bicycles in the van with us.

The car ride from our house to Holland takes about three hours. My sister was little. She wriggled, and squirmed, and complained the whole way. By the time we got to Grand Rapids, my dad looked worn out. It was only ten thirty in the morning!

Katie banged her hand into the edge of her seat belt buckle while we were playing "go fish." I guess she was mad at me because I was winning. My mom used a piece of tissue to stop Katie's finger from bleeding. We needed to find a drugstore quick.

The minute we got inside the drugstore, my dad and I could see we were in for it. My sister is crazy about stuffed toys. There was a whole shelf of stuffed animals in that place. We knew Katie would figure she was entitled to a present because she was hurt. Plus, her birthday was coming up the following month.

It happened that the drugstore was owned by a Dutch family. I later found out that over 10,000 people with Dutch kin were living in Grand Rapids by 1890. Because the Dutch settlers were good at making furniture, Grand Rapids became the furniture capital of America.

Anyway, as we had guessed, Katie went straight for those stuffed animals. She knew right away which one we had to buy for her.

"Daddy! Daddy!" she called, "You have to buy Jody, the Dutch mouse! He says he was born in Holland. He'll take us to the *Tulpen Feest*.

"The what?!" I thought I had wax in my ears.

"Don't ask!" said my dad, squeezing Jody's soft belly, as he caught the mouse in his big hand. A tear hung on Katie's cheek. Then she saw my dad was paying for Jody at the front counter. She turned to me with her hands on her hips and announced,

"*Tulpen Feest*, is Dutch for 'Tulip Festival' stupid!"

We got back into the van. Katie wanted to get Jody the mouse out of the paper bag right away. She stomped her foot and howled. My mom told her Jody could come out to play. But, first Katie's finger had to be bandaged. She could let me hold Jody if she wanted.

"Kevin will hurt him. He doesn't care about Jody," Katie said between sobs.

"No, no, sweetheart. Kevin will be very very careful with him, he promises. Don't you Kevin?"

I swore that I would.

I guess Katie didn't believe me. She watched me like a hawk. When our mother let go of her, she grabbed Jody off my lap like I was the enemy.

When we got to Holland, Jody told Katie where to go in "Hollmouse" (that's the language she says he speaks). Katie translated Jody's advice for my dad. It was simple enough, if we were willing to believe a stuffed mouse.

As we headed for 7th Street and Lincoln Avenue, our father said to Katie, "Would you mind asking Jody where he's taking us?"

"To see *DeZwann*. It means 'The Swan'." My sister answered triumphantly. "It's the oldest Dutch windmill in America. It's over 200 years old. They still make flour there!"

Our father sighed. He always liked to encourage us kids to be sure of ourselves. So we'd get a little lost. No big deal.

When we got onto 7th Street, we caught glimpses of the windmill. My sister bounced up and down in her seat. She made Jody dance on her knees.

"Jody can hardly wait Daddy! He wants to scamper through the 100,000 tulips they have here. He wants to ride on the *draalmolen* (merry-go-round) too."

It was a good thing Katie was tied down by her seatbelt. Otherwise there's no telling what might have happened.

My mom went ga ga over the tulips. Imagine what it was like being with her along the eight miles of tulip lanes that line the streets in downtown Holland!

After a while, Jodie and Katie had their fill of the children's zoo on Windmill Island and racing around *DeZwann*. Katie announced that we had to leave right away for the Dutch Village. She knew, or rather Jody knew, it was north on US 31.

I guess the Dutch Village looks just like the real Holland in Europe. The houses have **stepped gables** (the pointed ends of the houses look like stairs or steps).

This Dutch Village has brick streets that run along canals. There are pretty bridges across the water. One we went over was arched. It was made of brick. The road part was **planked** (made out of wood).

As we walked along the sea wall, we came to a café called The "Hungry Dutchman." It would have been a great place to eat if we hadn't already bought snacks from the other shops.

Then we found a place with a witches' scale - *Hexenwaag* in Dutch. This scale was made in 1708. My dad talked my mom into getting weighed. My mom wasn't crazy about this idea. A small crowd had already gathered to watch her.

My dad told my mom he likes her because she's a good sport. I noticed he wouldn't get on the scale. When she tried to pull him along after her, he said "Naw! I'm too heavy, Mary. I'd break it!"

I wasn't sure that was true. I don't think my mom believed it either because she said to my dad, "What a cop-out artist you are Mike!"

That afternoon, we found a bench next to the canal. We stopped there to eat some Dutch cheese and bread my parents had bought. We also had some cookies and a couple of Dutch chocolates.

Katie and Jody were playing near the bench. All of a sudden we heard a huge splash.

"I wonder what that was?" said my mom, turning around to look into the canal.

"Probably a big fish," joked my father.

"Maybe a Dutch whale!" I laughed.

My mother wasn't laughing. She had slipped out of her shoes and jumped into the canal. She was still wearing her blue jeans.

Katie had fallen in. She was thrashing around, bawling her head off. My mom caught hold of one of her skinny arms and pulled her back to the side of the canal. My dad lifted my sister back onto shore. I gave my mom a hand as she raised herself up onto the sea wall.

My sister was coughing and crying when we pulled her ashore. I stood by, feeling helpless and angry. Leave it to Katie to pull a stupid stunt like this! I was afraid she might die. How could a person drown in only four feet of water?!

My mom looked funny. My dad was bending over Katie, rubbing her back between the shoulder blades. A crowd of people had gathered around us.

I felt ashamed. Katie always did know how to turn a perfectly nice day into a drama. Fortunately she stopped coughing. Next she started to wail. A man stepped out of the crowd.

"I'm a doctor!" said the stranger. He leaned over my sister and examined her.

"Jody is drowning!" my sister sputtered. "He fell in the canal. I tried to get him. Please daddy, save him! Please save Jody!"

"We'll buy a new Jody," growled my father. He was in no mood to get soaking wet for a stuffed mouse.

A kind old man fished Jody out with his cane. The mouse was a little soggy. He had been floating belly-up, with a big grin on his face.

The doctor showed us to a nearby hotel where Katie and Jody could dry out. We stayed overnight. The Tulip Festival was scheduled to begin the following afternoon.

When we were sure that Katie was okay, we went back into the Dutch Village to do some more sightseeing. A lot of the houses there were brick, with clay tile roofs - just like in the old country. They also had an old-time wedding wagon and a mail wagon.

The *Klompen* (wooden shoe) dancers came out to perform to the music of the beautiful Amsterdam Street Organ.

Every fifteen minutes craftsmen showed how they made fudge, hand-carved shoes, or candles. My mom, Katie, and Jody the mouse, watched the candlemakers. My dad and I wanted some excitement. We went on the *Zweefmolen*, a neat swinging chair carousel they have there.

At dinnertime we found a real Dutch restaurant with a wood beam ceiling and open hearth fireplace . It was called the Queen's Inn. Part of the roof had been thatched by a Netherland thatcher. It was cool. My mom loved it because they served real Dutch food.

My mom knows I love history. She finds museums for me to visit wherever we go. The morning of the Tulip Festival, she took me to the Herrick Public Library and The Holland Museum to learn about how the early Dutch settlers lived. After that we visited the Cappon House. It was the home of Isaac Cappon. He was Holland's first mayor.

One neat thing I learned about was this guy named Engbertus van der Veen. He wrote **memoirs** (a personal account of hard times - kind of like my stories about travelling with my sister).

Engbertus was one of the first settlers. He left Amsterdam with his father in 1847. He wrote that when his family arrived in Holland, Michigan they were very upset because it was a wild, scary place.

It was "really a dense forest of big trees . . . the air was full of malaria caused by the swamp, stagnant water, and dirty waters of Black Lake - a place of sickness and death."*

The family built a fire. The "moaning sounds of the western pine, the night birds squawking and shrilly breaking into weird cries, the hooting of owls, and the croaking of a multitude of strange creatures . . ." frightened them.

*From *The Making of Michigan, 1820-1860: a Pioneer Anthology*. Ed. Justin L. Kestenbaum (Wayne State University Press, 1990), pp. 181-205.

This Engbertus guy's mom wanted to go back to Amsterdam right away. The family camped for two months. They were hoping a ship would come to take them home. Finally they realized they would have to stay in the terrifying wilderness.

Life in America must have been rough at first, but the Dutch were hard workers and very brave. In the Netherlands, there weren't many trees, so the people built their homes with brick. In America they learned how to build wooden houses and roads. This meant they had to learn how to chop down trees for lumber.

At first the Hollanders would chop all around the tree trunks. They didn't realize that a tree standing in the middle of a stump could fall in any direction. Sometimes trees fell on people's houses and crushed them.

The only roads were the Indian trails. The Dutch made "log bridges" across the low, wet spots in these trails. Engbertus didn't like the log roads much because, he says, "Riding over such a bridge in a lumber wagon drawn by oxen was a severe trial. The shaking made me sick in my stomach."

The new settlers didn't understand Indian ways. When the Hollanders saw **venison** (deer meat) hanging from trees, they thought nobody wanted it. They took the meat down and ate it up. This made the Indians mad. They had hung that meat out to cure, so it would taste better.

The Indians used to plant corn and beans before they went north to hunt. The Hollanders found the rich fields the Indians had left behind. They figured the Indians didn't want this land anymore. They divided up the corn and bean fields among themselves.

Then the Indians returned from the hunt. They must have been looking forward to some tasty corn on the cob. Imagine how annoyed they were when they saw those Dutchmen harvesting their food. I guess the Indians lost patience with their new neighbors. They sold all their land to the Dutch. Then they moved away.

The Tulip Festival opened that afternoon with Klomplen dancers. Katie danced with Jody in her arms. She was kicking the people next to us. My dad hoisted her up onto his shoulders.

After the dancing was over, the mayor and city council inspected the streets. They said that 8th Street was dirty.

Dutch men came out with pails of water. The pails were hung from wooden yokes across the men's shoulders. Dutch women scrubbed the pavements with brushes and brooms.

Katie and I both wanted a pair of wooden shoes like the ones these people were wearing. We could have bought them at the Dutch Village, but my dad said "no." I think he was afraid Katie would hurt someone while pretending to be a Klompen dancer in those hard shoes.

After the street scrubbing, there was a colorful Volksparade. Everyone dressed the way the early settlers did back in the 1800s.

When the parade was over, we got a map of the bike trails from the Chamber of Commerce.

My dad decided we should ride our bikes along South Shore Drive. This route runs beside Lake Macatawa to Macatawa Park. There we could see Big Red, the Macatawa Holland Harbor Lighthouse, and the beautiful shoreline of Lake Michigan.

Katie was exhausted. I wonder why. Luckily my dad has a child trailer for his bike. Katie was still small enough to ride in it that year. She and Jody climbed in and fell asleep. It's too bad they missed the best part of the trip.

We rode along the lake. It was filled with big boats. The houses along South Shore Drive are huge and very elegant. My mom said she'd need servants if we lived there.

When we got near the lighthouse, the hills were dotted with charming old homes. The place was full of cottages.

We locked up our bikes so we could walk out onto the white sand. My dad lifted my sleeping sister out of the trailer. She rubbed her eyes. She was grumpy. After a few minutes she realized that Jody was missing.

"Jody! Where's Jody?!" she wailed. Our poor father had to go back for the mouse. Katie hugged that stupid stuffed toy as though it were the most precious thing in the world.

There was a good wind blowing. The sun was warm on our faces. The sand felt cold on my bare toes when I thrust them underneath it. We could see up and down the beach and far out onto the lake.

The bright red lighthouse stood in the middle of a **shoal** (a narrow, shallow piece of land that sticks out into the water). I wanted to climb up into the tower to get a better view, but the lighthouse is private property. You can only see it with a guided tour. My dad said we'd have to come back. There's so much to see and do in this part of Michigan.

We rode our bikes back into downtown Holland. Katie and Jody slept in the trailer behind our father's bicycle. They never even woke up when my dad strapped them into their seat in the van.

My parents decided it would be "romantic" (yu-uck!) to drive south on US 31 a few miles to Saugatuck. That town is a colorful artist's colony on Lake Kalamazoo.

We got into Saugatuck as the sun was setting. The water was black, but the sky was a bright navy blue. You could still see red and gold reflections from the sun shimmering on the water's surface.

That night we had our dinner at The Mermaids. It was in the Dockside Marketplace, overlooking the water. We had a hard time deciding between this place and Coral Gables, another restaurant with a view of the water. I guess both of them have fireplaces. My mom wished we could come back in the winter and eat by the fire.

I wished we had time for the Star of Saugatuck boat cruise. This paddleboat boat ride would have taken us along the Kalamazoo River and out into Lake Michigan. Cool.

There were over 30 bed and breakfasts in Saugatuck. My parents finally chose one.

My sister woke up screaming in the middle of the night. "Mommy, Mommy!" she sobbed, "I dreamt I couldn't breathe."

"Well that's what happens when you jump into the canal after a stuffed mouse, and you don't know how to swim. Maybe next time you'll ask me or daddy to help you," said my mom.

"Maybe I should take swimming lessons," Katie suggested.

"Well that's okay with me. But, for now, if Jody falls into any more water - even a puddle you let me or daddy get him for you, okay?"

"Okay, Mommy," Katie replied with a yawn as she drifted back to sleep.

The next morning, after breakfast, we went down into the town to see what it was like. My sister wanted to pat the fat ducks and geese waddling along the street.

My dad took us for a Dune Schooner Ride that morning. Katie and Jody were wide awake and ready for action. This ride in a super jeep with roll bars and big balloon tires was exciting.

The ride took us into the large dunes of the Goshorn Lake area. We got to go through woodlands. We saw all kinds of wildlife.

There were three adorable baby raccoons. They were huddled together. When they saw the schooner, their eyes got very wide. They retreated sideways, shoulder to shoulder. They made clicking sounds as they moved away from us. I think they were trying to scare us so that we wouldn't realize how scared they were.

The schooner seated 20 people. Everyone took pictures. The scenery was awesome. The schooner glided over those dunes like they were nothing. Now that's a ride I'd like to go on again and again!

Katie and Jody couldn't stop talking about the dune ride, in "Hollmouse" of course. They did this all the way to Veldheer's Tulip Farm and DeKlomp.

Veldheer's has windmills and canals. I noticed my sister wisely kept clear of the water.

I was glad we had gone a little out of our way to visit this place. (Veldheer's is just north of Holland on US 31.) The bright blue sky really made the 2 million colorful tulips they had there pop out at you. My mom wished we could come back in July to see the summer gardens that bloom after the tulips are done.

The DeKlomp Delftware factory is the only place in the U.S. where they make the famous blue and white Dutch china. The china began to be produced in the Dutch city of Delft during the 13th century.

A beautiful Dutch girl dressed in a white lace shawl and **coiffe** (a cap that is like a hood) was painting plates and vases by hand.

My mom went wild in the gift shop. She bought a china clock and a flower vase. Naturally Katie had to have a blue and white Delft windmill. I really didn't want any of this china, even though I could see it was pretty.

Before leaving for home we visited the DeKlomp Wooden Shoe Factory. Katie and I still wanted wooden shoes. My dad said if we passed by one more place that sold wooden shoes, he would buy some. Lucky for us kids, you couldn't turn off US 31 for Grand Rapids without going by Holland's Original Wooden Shoe Factory.

Holland's Wooden Shoe Factory is a working museum. They still use antique equipment to make some of the shoes.

Katie saw it first. "Daddy! Daddy!" she shouted. "There it is! Stop!!"

My dad looked at my mom and shrugged sheepishly. We knew he was about to cave in.

When we got home, Katie refused to be separated from Jody, even for a moment. She chattered to him in Hollmouse and Klompen danced with him for hours on end.

Jody slept in Katie's bed. He joined us at the breakfast table every morning. I guess he liked jam and pancake syrup. Soon his fuzzy snout was sticky. I had to read the comics to Jody.

"If he doesn't understand English, why am I reading to him?" I asked my sister.

"Jody speaks perfect English. He just doesn't feel like it," she snapped. " In fact, Jody speaks every language there is."

This was the beginning of many years of having Jody as our official family "interpreter."

THE END

Join the FUN

Get Your **FREE** Subscription to

Jody's Travel Quarterly ©

a Newsletter for Kids

Call 1 888-ask JODY

1 888-275 5639